Mountains

by Sheila Anderson

Lerner Books · London · New York · Minneapolis

What is a **mountain?**

It is a kind of **landform.**

A mountain is land that rises towards the sky.

Mountains are taller than
the land around them.

There are mountains in the
ocean. These are **islands.**

Many **volcanoes** are mountains.

Some mountains have
pointed tops.

Some mountains have
rounded tops.

Some mountains are rocky.

Many mountains have snow
on top.

Animals live on mountains.

Plants grow on mountains.

People live on mountains.

People **climb** mountains.

There are many things to
do on a mountain.

Would you like to explore a mountain?

rain
shadow

Rain Shadow

Do you know what a rain shadow is? It is the area on one side of a mountain that gets very little rain.

Mountains help to make rain shadows. When clouds blow over mountains, they cool. The water in the clouds falls as rain or snow.

By the time the cloud is over the mountain, most of the water is gone. So the other side of the mountain gets very little rain. It becomes a rain shadow.

Mountain Facts

 The outer part of the Earth is called the crust. Some mountains are formed when two pieces of the Earth's crust push against each other. They push the land up, making a mountain.

 Some mountains are formed when hot lava from deep within the Earth comes out of a crack in the Earth's crust. It flows up and out and then cools, forming a mound.

The world's highest mountain is Mount Everest. It is in Asia and is 8,848 metres high.

 The highest mountain in the United Kingdom is Ben Nevis. It is in Scotland and is 1,344 m high.

 The air high up in the sky is cooler than the air lower down, so some mountain tops are cold and have snow all year round.

Glossary

 climb – to go up, down or over using hands and feet

 islands – pieces of land that have water on all sides

 landform – a natural feature of the Earth's surface

 mountain – an area of land that rises to a great height

 volcanoes – breaks in the Earth's surface where hot, molten (melted) rock called lava flows out

Index

The photographs in this book are reproduced with the permission of: © Mary Liz Austin/Image Bank/Getty Images, pp 2, 22 (second from bottom); © Prisma/SuperStock, pp 3, 22 (middle); © Peter Van Rhijn/SuperStock, p 4; © Rod Barbee/Visuals Unlimited, p 5; © Dick Roberts/ Visuals Unlimited, pp 6, 22 (second from top); © age fotostock/SuperStock, pp 7, 11, 17, 22 (bottom); © Gary Brettnacher/SuperStock, p 8; PhotoDisc Royalty-Free by Getty Images, pp 9, 12; © Steve Vidler/SuperStock, p 10; © istockphoto.com/Kateryna Govorushchenko, p 13; © istockphoto.com/Kateryna Govorushchenko, p 14; © Pierre Jacques/Getty Images, pp 15, 22 (top); © Photononstop/SuperStock, p 16.

Front Cover: © Richard Price/Taxi/Getty Images.
Illustration on p 18 by Laura Westlund/Independent Picture Service.

First published in the United Kingdom in 2010 by
Lerner Books,
Dalton House,
60 Windsor Avenue,
London SW19 2RR

Website address: www.lernerbooks.co.uk

This edition was updated and edited for UK publication by Discovery Books Ltd.,
First Floor, 2 College Street, Ludlow, Shropshire SY8 1AN

British Library Cataloguing in Publication Data

Anderson, Sheila
Mountains. - 2nd ed. - (First step nonfiction. Landforms)
1. Mountains - Juvenile literature 2. Mountain ecology -
Juvenile literature
I. Title
551.4'32

ISBN-13: 978 0 7613 4367 7

Printed in China

First published in the United States of America in 2008
Text copyright © 2008 by Lerner Publishing Group, Inc.